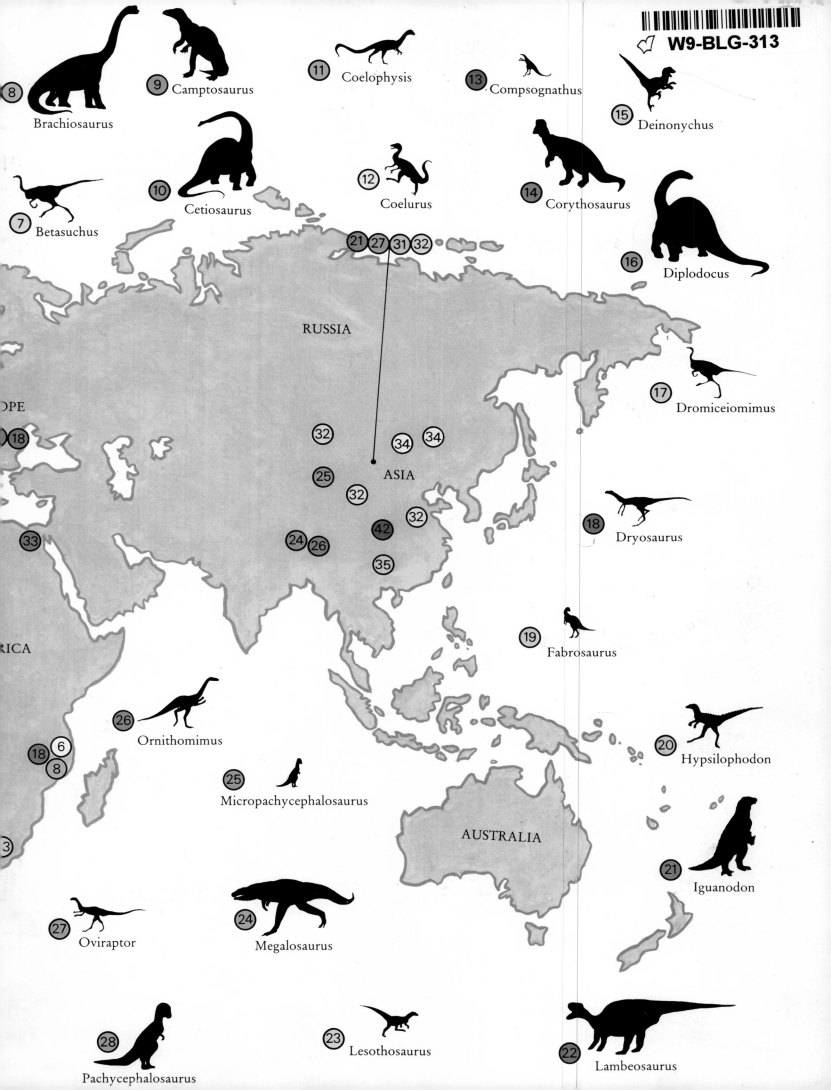

8 Brachiosaurus

9 Camptosaurus

11 Coelophysis

13 Compsognathus

15 Deinonychus

14 Corythosaurus

10 Cetiosaurus

12 Coelurus

7 Betasuchus

16 Diplodocus

RUSSIA

17 Dromiceiomimus

21 27 31 32

OPE

18

32

34 34

25

32

ASIA

33

32

42

32

24 26

18 Dryosaurus

35

19 Fabrosaurus

RICA

26 Ornithomimus

20 Hypsilophodon

18 6

8

25 Micropachycephalosaurus

AUSTRALIA

3

21 Iguanodon

27 Oviraptor

24 Megalosaurus

28 Pachycephalosaurus

23 Lesothosaurus

22 Lambeosaurus

Designed by Brigitte Willgoss
Celia Chester
Edited by Debbie Lines

ISBN 0 86112 460 X
© BRIMAX BOOKS LTD 1988. All rights reserved
Published by BRIMAX BOOKS ENGLAND 1988
Third printing 1988
Printed in Portugal

Dinosaurs

Written by Stephen Attmore
Illustrated by David A. Hardy
Diagrams by David A. Hardy and Brian Rhoden

Contents

Brimax Books · Newmarket · England

What was a dinosaur?

For 160 million years dinosaurs were the largest and most frightening animals that ever lived on Earth. Some weighed almost as much as a blue whale, about 130 tonnes (127 tons) – yet others were no bigger than a chicken. However, dinosaurs died out 65 million years ago.

The term 'dinosaur' was first used in 1841. It is taken from the Greek word 'deinos' meaning 'terrible' and 'saur' meaning 'lizard'. The dinosaur's ancestors were reptiles that ran on their hind legs. Many of these reptiles looked like crocodiles with their legs held out sideways. Others had limbs that were underneath the body so that they could run faster. Some developed large hind legs and short front legs. They used their hind legs for running and their front legs for grasping food.

tyrannosaurus rex

How to say the names of the dinosaurs in this book:

allosaurus	al-lo-sor-us	mastodonsaurus	mass-toe-don-sor-us
anatosaurus	an-at-oh-sor-us	megalosaurus	meg-a-lo-sor-us
ankylosaurus	an-kil-oh-sor-us	micropachycephalosaurus	my-kroh-pak-ee-sef-alo-sor-us
apatosaurus	a-pat-oh-sor-us	ornithomimus	or-nith-oh-mime-us
archaeopteryx	ark-ee-op-ter-iks	ornithosuchus	or-nith-oh-sook-us
barosaurus	barrow-sor-us	oviraptor	oh-vee-rap-tor
betasuchus	bee-ta-sook-us	pachycephalosaurus	pak-ee-sef-alo-sor-us
brachiosaurus	brak-ee-oh-sor-us	parasaurolophus	pah-rah-sor-ol-oh-fus
camptosaurus	kamp-toe-sor-us	placodus	plak-oh-dus
cetiosaurus	ket-ee-oh-sor-us	plateosaurus	plat-ee-oh-sor-us
coelophysis	see-lo-fy-sis	plesiosaur	ple-see-oh-sor
coelurus	see-loor-us	podopteryx	pod-op-ter-iks
compsognathus	komp-so-na-thus	protoceratops	pro-toe-ser-ah-tops
corythosaurus	korr-ee-tho-sor-us	psittacosaurus	sit-a-ko-sor-us
cynognathus	sino-na-thus	pteranodon	ter-a-no-don
deinonychus	die-non-ike-us	pterosaur	ter-oh-sor
diplodocus	dip-loh-doe-kus	quetzalcoatlus	kwet-zal-kote-lus
dromiceiomimus	drom-ick-eye-oh-mime-us	rhamphorhynchus	ram-for-in-kus
dryosaurus	dri-oh-sor-us	saltoposuchus	salt-oh-poss-ook-us
elasmosaurus	ee-laz-mo-sor-us	saurolophus	sor-ol-oh-fus
euparkeria	you-park-er-ee-ah	saurornithoides	sor-or-nith-oy-dees
fabrosaurus	fab-ro-sor-us	sinosaurus	sy-no-sor-us
hypselosaurus	hip-sel-oh-sor-us	spinosaurus	spy-no-sor-us
hypsilophodon	hip-sil-off-od-on	staurikosaurus	stor-ik-oh-sor-us
iguanodon	ih-gwan-oh-don	stegoceras	steg-oss-er-as
kronosaurus	kro-no-sor-us	stegosaurus	steg-o-sor-us
lagosuchus	lag-oh-sook-us	styracosaurus	sty-rak-oh-sor-us
lesothosaurus	less-oh-toe-sor-us	teratosaurus	ter-a-toe-sor-us
lambeosaurus	lam-ee-oh-sor-us	triceratops	try-ser-a-tops
lystrosaurus	lie-stro-sor-us	tyrannosaurus	tie-ran-oh-sor-us
maiasaura	my-er-sor-ah		

When did dinosaurs roam the Earth?

The history of life on Earth is divided into three parts. It is the middle section that is known as the Age of Dinosaurs. Dinosaurs began to appear on Earth about 225 million years ago. They continued to breed and adapt to their environment over the next 160 million years.

If one year represents the time that there has been life on Earth, then the first dinosaurs did not appear until around December 8th and died out December 24th. The first human beings were born late in the evening of December 31st.

euparkeria

pterosaur

sinosaurus

TRIASSIC PERIOD

JURASSIC PERIOD

210 million years ago   200   190   180

archaeopteryx   brachiosaurus   allosaurus

130   140   150   160   170

iguanodon   quetzalcoatlus   tyrannosaurus

CRETACEOUS PERIOD

120   110   100   90

ankylosaurus

40   50   60   70   80

HERE AND NOW

Past   Future

30   20   10 million years ago

How dinosaurs evolved

Dinosaurs evolved from swimming reptiles (1) who hunted their prey in water. They swam by waggling their long, strong tails. To set off they pushed down and back with their hind legs which were longer and more powerful than their front limbs.

Over a long period of time – several million years – some of these reptiles took to living on the land mainly to find new sources of food and to avoid predatory fish. Most could not walk as upright as a dog, but used their limbs to lift their bodies off the ground (a). They probably looked like trotting crocodiles (2). At feeding and breeding times they returned to the water.

From such reptiles came creatures like the tiny **euparkeria** (3) which was only 1 m (3¼ ft) long. It walked on land on all fours lifting its body higher off the ground (b). As its short front legs made running difficult, the euparkeria sprinted by

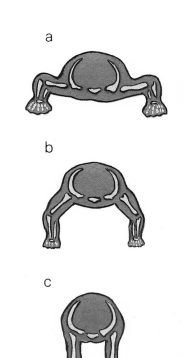

a

b

c

evolution of hip position

8

rearing up on its long hind legs. It used its very long tail to balance as it darted from place to place.

The **lagosuchus** (4) was given its name by scientists because of the speed at which it moved. Lagosuchus means 'hare crocodile'. This small creature also walked on all fours but ran on its hind legs only. Both the euparkeria and the lagosuchus were flesh-eating creatures, feeding on animals smaller than themselves. The **ornithosuchus** (5) was another flesh-eating hunter. It was about 3 m (9¾ ft) long.

True dinosaurs had a much improved stance with hind legs held straight down below the body (c). This helped dinosaurs like **staurikosaurus** (6) to outrun both prey and rivals. These dinosaurs were therefore more dangerous than their reptile ancestors. It is likely that the number of dinosaurs on Earth increased at a much quicker rate than other animals because they could run faster. The largest plant-eating dinosaurs could escape from predators and the meat-eating dinosaurs could catch and kill the slower moving animals.

key
1 lizard-like reptile
2 crocodile-like ancestor of the dinosaur
3 euparkeria
4 lagosuchus
5 ornithosuchus
6 staurikosaurus

Life in the Triassic Period

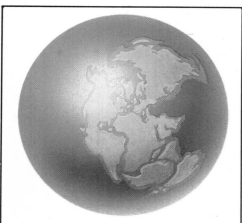

Earth – 225 million years ago, at the start of the Triassic Period.

As the picture shows, Earth was very different when the first dinosaurs lived on it. The land masses were joined together. Dinosaurs and other animals could roam for thousands of miles in search of food.

The first part of the Age of Dinosaurs is known as the Triassic Period. This lasted for about 35 million years and began about 225 million years ago.

Perhaps the most amazing thing about life on Earth in the Age of Dinosaurs was the climate. Everywhere was warm – all the time. Imagine summer lasting for millions of years. Although there were some mountains and volcanoes, most of the land was flat. There were many marshes and swamps, covered with a variety of trees and plants. One unusual tree called pleuromeia was 2 m (7 ft) high and had tufts of leaves near the top of its thick stalk.

It was during the Triassic Period that the first dinosaurs appeared. Reptiles began to adjust to a way of life on land. Along the shores waddled reptiles such as the **placodus**. This animal lived on land but returned to the sea in search of food. The **lystrosaurus** was a mammal-like reptile. It looked like a

baby hippo. The **cynognathus** was a hairy carnivore (meateater) about the size of a wolf.

The mammal-like reptiles were gradually replaced by early dinosaurs such as **euparkeria** and the **saltoposuchus** which was only 87 cm (2¾ ft) long. It ran on the toes of its hind legs, using its very long tail to help it balance. The **lagosuchus** was a small speedy, flesh-eating dinosaur.

Towards the end of the Triassic Period larger dinosaurs evolved. One of the biggest was a herbivore (plant-eater) called **plateosaurus**. The **ornithosuchus, staurikosaurus, teratosaurus** and **sinosaurus** were all carnivores. Above their heads gliding reptiles moved from tree to tree and the first **pterosaurs** flew by on skin wings.

key		
1 placodus	6 lagosuchus	11 sinosaurus
2 lystrosaurus	7 plateosaurus	12 gliding lizard
3 cynognathus	8 ornithosuchus	13 pterosaur
4 euparkeria	9 staurikosaurus	
5 saltoposuchus	10 teratosaurus	

Life in the Jurassic Period

Earth – 165 million years ago, during the Jurassic Period.

The continents slowly drifted apart over millions of years. Fossil bones of the same type of dinosaur are now being uncovered in different continents around the world.

The Jurassic Period lasted for 50 million years. There was a great increase in the number of animals in the water, on land and in the air. By the end of the Period, dinosaurs were the rulers of the animal kingdom. Some had grown to enormous sizes and weights. The ground shook as they moved along.

The climate everywhere was warm and moist. There were coral reefs and lagoons along many coasts. Plants grew more thickly, including many cycads (palm-like plants with coloured fruits and cones).

A variety of dinosaurs evolved to feed on the many plants available. Small dinosaurs munched the fungi and ferns at ground level. Slim dinosaurs chewed the leaves a little higher up. The **dryosaurus** was one of the biggest of these. The **camptosaurus** and **stegosaurus** could rear up on their hind legs to strip leaves off the lower branches of the taller trees. Giant dinosaurs like **diplodocus, brachiosaurus** and **cetiosaurus** ate the leaves too high for the others to reach.

There were also many hunters on the prowl. **Coelurus** was about the length of an adult human. It used its long hind legs for speedy running. Perhaps this scavenger tore flesh off other dinosaurs and mammals killed by larger carnivores such as the **allosaurus**.

Above the heads of the ground-living creatures flapped 'winged dinosaurs'. They had fragile wings of skin and bone. When **archaeopteryx** and **rhamphorhynchus** took to the air, they probably flew slowly and clumsily. They were too big to fly far.

key
1 dryosaurus
2 camptosaurus
3 stegosaurus
4 diplodocus
5 brachiosaurus
6 cetiosaurus
7 coelurus
8 allosaurus
9 archaeopteryx
10 rhamphorhynchus

Life in the Cretaceous Period

Earth – 100 million years ago, in the middle of the Cretaceous Period.
The continents are further apart. Seas separate the land masses and the climate is becoming more varied.

This was the last period in the Age of Dinosaurs. It lasted 70 million years, ending around 65 million years ago. During this time dinosaurs reached their peak and then mysteriously vanished from the face of the Earth.

In the Cretaceous Period many modern types of animal and plant appeared for the first time. There was a much greater variety of plants and trees. Flowering plants multiplied and spread. The climate was warm and wet ranging from very hot at the Equator to warm in the north.

There were many more plant-eating dinosaurs than meat-eaters. These evolved with teeth designed for chewing the new tough-leaved plants. They ranged in size from small two-footed dinosaurs to four-legged giants. The **micropachycephalosaurus** of China has one of the longest names but one of the shortest bodies of any dinosaur. Its

body was about 50 cm (20 ins) long. At the other end of the scale, the **apatosaurus** was still making the ground shake as it plodded across the plains of North America. This huge dinosaur was probably 21 m (70 ft) from nose to tip of tail.

Each creature had its own special feeding ground. The armour-plated **ankylosaurus** kept to higher, drier land. Duckbills such as the **corythosaurus** and **parasaurolophus** ate so much that they cleared areas completely. **Triceratops** roamed the plains in herds while **hypsilophodon** lived in forest glades. This left room for the ostrich dinosaurs like **betasuchus**. The massive **tyrannosaurus rex** fed on dead or injured dinosaurs.

Overhead flew the largest pterosaur, quetzalcoatlus at 12 m (39 ft) from wing tip to wing tip. The smaller **pteranodon** of North America had a wingspan of 8 m (26 ft). It spent most of its life in the air. There were also some species of true birds. **Gulls** and **wader birds** appeared for the first time during the Cretaceous Period.

key	
1	micropachycephalosaurus
2	apatosaurus
3	ankylosaurus
4	corythosaurus
5	parasaurolophus
6	triceratops
7	hypsilophodon
8	betasuchus
9	tyrannosaurus rex
10	pteranodon
11	gulls and waders

Family Life

Fossil eggs, nests and young found recently tell us about how dinosaurs produced and raised their babies. When mating time drew near, males probably fought each other for females. First they threatened, then they banged heads or slashed with their clawed feet. Male dinosaurs with loud voices or large crests probably showed them off to attract their mates.

After mating, female dinosaurs laid eggs. Some females may have covered their eggs with sand and left them to hatch in the sun. Others built nests with raised mud rims and brooded their eggs as chickens do. It is possible that some females carried live young inside them, as many mammals do.

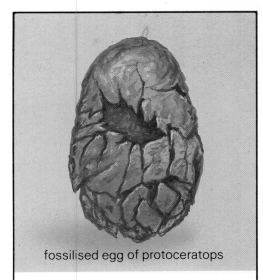

fossilised egg of protoceratops

A protoceratops' egg had ridges and wrinkles. When uncovered recently, the fossilised egg was red-brown.

Protoceratops laid eggs in hollows dug in sand. Each female laid a clutch of 12 or more, with the eggs' narrow ends facing inward. Very large clutches of eggs suggest that two females shared the nest.

The young protoceratops then hatched. Nearly all dinosaurs came from eggs. The eggs were warmed by the sun, mother's body or rotting leaves until they hatched.

The picture below shows a female **maiasaura** bringing food for her small hatchlings. She continued to feed her young until they could safely look for food on their own.

Certain dinosaurs bred in groups on hillsides. The adults shared the task of guarding the young. When old enough to look for their own food, these young dinosaurs were often protected in the herd by the adults. Many baby dinosaurs probably did not survive long enough to become fully developed. They were attacked and killed by carnivorous animals. Some adults killed their young if they were sick or wounded. However, a few dinosaurs may have lived for 100 years or more.

How big was a dinosaur egg? A baby hypselosaurus emerged from an egg 25 cm (10 ins) long and weighed approximately 1 kg (2.2 lb). It grew to an adult length of 12 m (40 ft) and weighed 10 tonnes, 10,000 times its birthweight! Some adult dinosaurs were even bigger and heavier.

hen's egg and hypselosaurus egg shown to scale.

Little and large

The biggest dinosaurs were the largest animals that ever lived on land. Each had a huge, barrel-shaped body, four thick legs, a long neck with a small head and a very long tail. Despite their massive size, they were gentle giants. They ate leaves and plants.

Here you can see the tallest, the longest and the heaviest dinosaurs.

Not all dinosaurs were large – some were little. Indeed, some types of dinosaurs were smaller than you.

1 **Micropachycephalosaurus** was only 50 cm (20 ins) long. Its name means 'tiny thick-headed lizard'.

2 **Compsognathus** was smaller than a chicken. It was 60 cm (2 ft) long and weighed only 3 kg (6½ lb).

3 **Lesothosaurus** was about the size of a duck. It was about 90 cm (3 ft) long.

4 **Diplodocus** was the longest ever dinosaur. One set of fossil bones had a total length of 26.6 m (87½ ft). That is about the same length as 16 men and women laid end to end!

5 **Barosaurus** was probably the tallest. Although not as long overall as the diplodocus, this dinosaur had a very long neck. The longest of its neck bones was nearly 1 m (3 ft).

6 **Brachiosaurus** was the heaviest dinosaur. Adults weighed over 77 tonnes (85 tons). In 1979 American bone-hunters uncovered the fossilised remains of a monster. They gave it the nickname 'ultrasaurus'. Its weight was estimated to be the same as 30 large elephants.

Lizard-hips and bird-hips

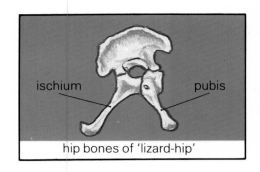

hip bones of 'lizard-hip'

In 1887 an English scientist named Henry Seeley introduced a new grouping among dinosaurs. He divided them into two orders, lizard-hips and bird-hips, according to the shape of their hip bones.

All animals need a framework of bone and muscle to support them as they move. Some dinosaurs had bones which were solid and heavy while others had hollow, light bones. The dinosaur's spine bore the strains and stresses of walking, running, feeding and fighting. The spine consists of bones or segments known as vertebrae. The number of these varied depending on the dinosaur's size and shape. As a rule, the hind legs were larger and stronger than the forelimbs ('arms'). The main weight of the body rested on the hind legs and was supported by the hip bones. It is the shape of this hip girdle which places dinosaurs into one of the two groups.

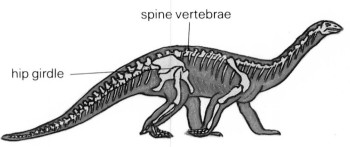

partial skeleton of 'lizard-hip'

'Lizard-hips' had a hip girdle arranged like those of lizards, crocodiles and other reptiles. The largest and fiercest dinosaurs belonged to this group. The four-legged giants barosaurus and brachiosaurus were 'lizard-hip' dinosaurs as were all the two-legged carnivores, such as **tyrannosaurus** (1) and megalosaurus.

Plateosaurus (2) walked on all fours but probably reared up to eat leaves high up, using its 'arms' as a prop.

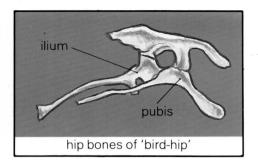

ilium

pubis

hip bones of 'bird-hip'

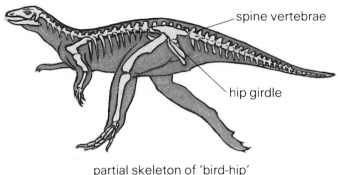

spine vertebrae

hip girdle

partial skeleton of 'bird-hip'

types of hip girdle (above and on opposite page) to see the difference.

'Bird-hip' dinosaurs did not evolve until some way into the Triassic Period. There was a wide range of species among the 'bird-hips'. Some walked on two legs, such as the **hypsilophodon** (3) and **fabrosaurus** (4). Others walked on all fours. Stegosaurus and ankylosaurus lumbered along, feeding on low-lying plants. 'Bird-hip' dinosaurs had an extra bone forming a tip to the lower jaw. Many had a horny beak, strong teeth and cheek pouches. All of them were herbivores.

Fabrosaurus was one of the first 'bird-hips'. This small animal was about 1 m (3¼ ft) long. Hypsilophodon was a fast runner, using its great speed to avoid predators.

The second order of dinosaurs is known as the 'bird-hips'. This is because their hip bones are arranged in the same way as those of a bird. Look at the drawings of the two

Plant-eaters

Most dinosaurs were plant-eaters. There was plenty of vegetation for them all. These dinosaurs had teeth like pegs. When these weak teeth wore down, new teeth grew to replace them.

Dinosaurs like **stegosaurus** (1) could eat enormous amounts of vegetation. As it had weak teeth it probably fed mainly on soft plants. The **iguanodon** (2) could rear up on its hind legs to strip leaves and twigs off the trees. It had large, grinding teeth in its upper and lower jaws. **Diplodocus** (3) had no trouble reaching the top of a tree.

Plant-eating dinosaurs probably had a keen sense of smell. This warned them when any predator was approaching. Although they could not move quickly, they had 'weapons' that came in useful in a fight. Iguanodons had a spiky thumb on each forelimb which served as daggers when it was attacked. The stegosaurus had body armour for protection against attackers. It also had at least four heavy spikes on its tail. These became a hefty weapon when it whipped its tail from side to side. A bull (adult male) diplodocus also lashed out with its tail. If that failed to deter the predator, it would rear up, using its tail as a prop, and bring down its front legs (as an elephant does to crush a tiger).

Apatosaurus was another giant plant-eating dinosaur. It is also called brontosaurus, which means 'thunder lizard'. This name comes from the sound it probably made as its feet thumped on the ground. The mouth of this enormous beast was quite small. Its head was no wider than its neck. The apatosaurus must have munched almost non-stop to provide enough food to satisfy its tremendous appetite.

When a predator approached, apatosaurus moved into water. If the predator came into the water after it, the giant dinosaur moved to deeper water. It could go in quite deep, up to its shoulders in the water. There were a lot of water plants so it did not have to stop eating.

nostril opening above eye

eye

24 peg-shaped teeth

apatosaurus skull

(actual size)

stomach stone used to aid digestion

Those dinosaurs with very weak teeth may have swallowed stones. These helped to grind food to a pulp in the dinosaur's stomach. The muscles in the stomach walls churned the stones and food together. Birds today swallow small stones and grit for a similar purpose.

Meat-eaters

Imagine the scene during the Age of Dinosaurs when one of the huge dinosaurs is faced with its fearsome enemy, a carnivore. A fierce battle follows. 'Gentle giant' versus 'mighty mauler'. The attacker is smaller but has razor-sharp teeth in its powerful jaws. It has talons in its feet. With a combination of tooth and claw, the carnivore attacks and can kill a dinosaur much bigger and heavier than itself.

In the scene below the meat-eater, **allosaurus** (1), is attacking a giant plant-eater, **brachiosaurus** (2). Another smaller carnivore, **megalosaurus** (3) is ripping flesh from a dead dinosaur. Scientists believe that the megalosaurus weighed 900 kg (1 ton). It had very sharp teeth and strong curved claws. No wonder plant-eaters ran into the water to escape!

All meat-eating dinosaurs walked and ran around on their hind legs. Many of these speedy runners had a stiffened tail. This helped them to balance on their hind legs – like a seesaw. Only the larger carnivores, like megalosaurus, allosaurus, ceratosaurus and tyrannosaurus, were a real threat to the plant-eaters. Some of the meat-eaters were no bigger than a chicken. One dinosaur, deinonychus ('terrible claw'), had formidable weapons in the shape of the claws on its feet (a). It would leap and slash at prey with all four feet.

The teeth of the meat-eaters were sharp, triangular and often serrated (b), enabling them to bite off chunks of flesh to swallow whole.

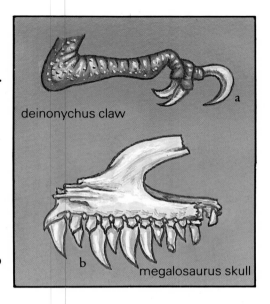

deinonychus claw

b   megalosaurus skull

Tyrannosaurus rex was king of the meat-eaters. It was 12 m (39 ft) long and was as heavy as an African elephant – 6.4 tonnes (7 tons). Because of its size, the tyrannosaurus was not the fastest carnivore that lived in the dinosaur world. Probably, tyrannosaurus preferred to eat carrion (dead animals). If it managed to catch live prey, its teeth might have snapped off during a fight and it needed these for tearing off lumps of flesh. The sharp claws on its hind feet were like carving knives and made powerful weapons. Strangely, it had tiny arms that were too weak to be of any use in a fight and too short to lift food to its mouth. This huge beast had eye sockets larger than your head!

Plates, spikes and horns

Those land-living dinosaurs unable to escape the speedy carnivores needed some form of protection. Some developed bony plates, while others sprouted horns or frills.

In the Jurassic Period, **stegosaurus** had two rows of pointed, bony plates along its back from neck to tail. The largest of these was 75 cm (2½ ft) high and about the same across. These may have served as a form of body heating, drawing heat from the sun, but they also made the stegosaurus look bigger. On its tail were at least four heavy spikes. Its back legs were twice as high as its front legs. Plated dinosaurs like stegosaurus died out because a carnivore's claws and fangs could pierce the areas of skin unprotected by plates.

In the Cretaceous Period, creatures known as 'reptilian tanks' replaced the plated dinosaurs. Tough skin covered flexible bony slabs and spikes, protecting all the upper parts of the beast's body. **Ankylosaurus** was the largest of these spiky dinosaurs. When attacked, it probably drew its head in and got as close to the ground as it could, to protect its soft underside from attack – as the armadillo does today. Its bony tail club made a useful weapon. Spiky dinosaurs had small teeth and weak jaws. They fed on soft plants and insects.

The horned dinosaurs evolved later in the Cretaceous Period. Although they looked fearsome, these plant-eaters were harmless unless provoked. Some were covered in horns and spikes, others had very long frills. They ranged from creatures lighter than an adult human to monsters twice as long as a rhinoceros and as heavy as a large elephant. Their ancestor was probably the **psittacosaurus** (1). This 'parrot lizard' had short bony plates jutting back from the sides of the head.

The **styracosaurus** (2) had one straight nose horn and six long spikes jutting backward from the skull. The spikes were an adaptation of the bony neck frill of the **triceratops** (3). Measuring 9 m (30 ft) from beak to tip of tail, the triceratops was one of the largest and one of the last of the horned dinosaurs. Two horns, each 1 m (3¼ ft) long, grew from its forehead and a third was seated on the nose. The back of its skull spread out to form a bony collar which protected the dinosaur's neck when its head was raised. When a determined triceratops put its head down and charged, even the tyrannosaurus probably ran away!

Horned dinosaurs probably lived in herds, and it is likely that the adults protected the young from attackers by forming an outward-facing ring. This would have stopped any predator from getting too close. The horned dinosaurs would have used their horns as defence weapons.

Head-bangers

'Boneheads' were two-footed dinosaurs with thick skulls. They may have evolved from the same ancestor as horned dinosaurs, the psittacosaurus. Herds of 'boneheads' roamed hills in North America and Asia in the Cretaceous Period. Each herd had a strong male as its leader. Many munched leaves, seeds, fruit and possibly insects.

Male 'boneheads' had thicker skulls than females. The roof of the skull was expanded to form a dome. **Stegoceras** had a brain the size of a hen's egg. Yet that brain was inside a bony dome five times thicker than your skull.

The biggest 'bonehead' of them all was **pachycephalosaurus** whose skull was 22 cm (8½ ins) thick. That is 20 times thicker than a human skull. Bony spikes jutted upwards from above the snout and bony knobs rimmed the back of the head.

Why did 'boneheads' have such thick skulls? The answer may be that males would fight over the females or to decide who would lead the herd. Crash! They banged their heads together. Probably they did not fight to kill. 'Boneheads' may also have used their thick skulls to drive away predators.

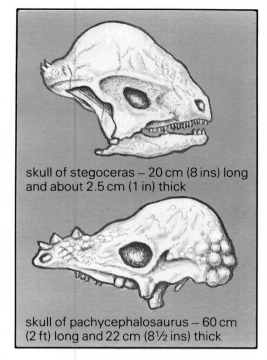

skull of stegoceras – 20 cm (8 ins) long and about 2.5 cm (1 in) thick

skull of pachycephalosaurus – 60 cm (2 ft) long and 22 cm (8½ ins) thick

When two male stegoceras crashed head-on, there was no damage to the brain or backbone because the thick bone acted as a pad to absorb the blow.

Duck-billed dinosaurs

As 'boneheads' roamed hills, a strange relative browsed among conifer trees in northern lands. These dinosaurs walked on three-toed hind legs and used their long, heavy tail as a prop when resting or feeding. Both arms had four webbed fingers.

Duckbills got their name from their toothless beaks. At the back of the mouth, however, were hundreds of teeth designed to grind tough leaves. **Anatosaurus** had about 1000 teeth in its wide jaws. It was one of the largest duckbills – up to 13 m (42½ ft) long. Loose skin on its flat face could be blown up to help it make a loud bellowing call.

anatosaurus

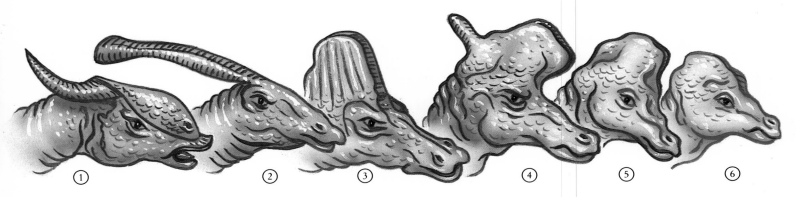

① ② ③ ④ ⑤ ⑥

Some duck-billed dinosaurs had a crest on top of the head. Different kinds had different crests. **Saurolophus** (1) had a spiky crest and a frill at the back of its skull. It may have been able to blow up skin balloons along the length of its face. **Parasaurolophus** (2) had a 1.8 m (6 ft) horn curving backward from the top of its head. **Corythosaurus** (3) had a tall, rounded crest like a helmet.

Why did these duck-billed dinosaurs have a crest? It was not for head-banging. It was simply to help them recognise their own kind. The **lambeosaurus** males (4) had larger crests than the females (5) and their young (6). At mating time the head crests, bellowing calls or skin flaps blown up like balloons, probably helped males and females of the same species to find each other.

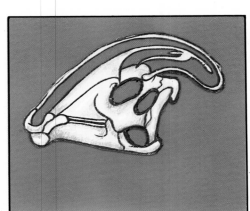

Diagram of skull of a female parasaurolophus. When these duck-billed dinosaurs called to one another their long air passages (in red) made a sound like a bugle or hunting horn.

Strange beasts

'Ostrich' dinosaurs

These strange beasts lived late in the Age of Dinosaurs. They looked something like ostriches without feathers, with their long necks and long legs. They used their arms to gather fruits and to tear open ants' nests. When they walked or ran, they held their tail out stiffly level with their back. These dinosaurs had good eyesight. If an enemy came near, they ran away quickly.

'Ostrich' dinosaurs had light, hollow bones. They were around 3.5 m (11½ ft) in length. More than half the length of **ornithomimus** was its tail. This strange beast lived in forests and swamps in North America, feeding on lizards and mammals, insects and fruit, and sometimes eggs.

ornithomimus

Oviraptor was also an 'ostrich' dinosaur but was known as the 'egg thief'. It had a toothless beak and strong jaws. It used its lower jaw to crush hard food, such as tough egg shells.

The egg thief's fingers had long bones and strong, curved claws. The first finger claw is about 8 cm (3 ins) long.

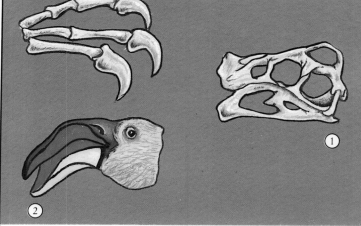

Oviraptor had a short, deep skull (1). It looks like no other known dinosaur's, yet it is similar in shape to the head of a flamingo (2).

Feathered dinosaur

Archaeopteryx looked like a cross between a bird and a reptile. It was about the size of a crow and had feathered wings. It had a toe which pointed backward on each foot, like today's birds. It probably could not fly far but it was a fast runner, possibly quick enough to catch flying insects. Like reptiles, this strange beast's jaws were lined with tiny teeth. Three clawed fingers sprouted from each 'feathered arm'.

archaeopteryx

Baby hippo?

Lystrosaurus was a mammal-like reptile. It led a life similar to that of the modern hippopotamus. It wallowed in mud, eating water plants. It was small – only about 80 cm (2½ ft). To build a den it scraped a hole with its powerful front legs. A single pair of fangs stuck out from its snout. Fossil bones were found in southern Africa and the Antarctic. This suggests that these two continents were joined together in the Triassic Period (see picture of Earth – page 10).

lystrosaurus

mastodonsaurus

Giant frog?

Mastodonsaurus lived all its life under water. It looked like a huge frog and was over 3 m (10 ft) long. Its jaws were armed with sharp teeth. Short legs and a short tail show that this beast preferred swimming to walking.

Monsters of the deep

The largest dinosaurs were so huge that they could not move very well on land. Their enormous body and neck was supported by four short legs. Imagine carrying round a load weighing 77 tonnes (85 tons)! **Brachiosaurus** spent most of its time in water which helped to support its tremendous body weight. It could not swim so it would walk slowly out from the bank or shore up to shoulder height. The brachiosaurus was safe from predators while it stayed in the water. There were plenty of water plants to eat. It was probably content to stand for hours in the water. It is a curious feature of the brachiosaurus that its nostrils were on top of its head. It was thought at one time that the brachiosaurus would breathe through them when in deep water but it is now known that the pressure of the water at that depth would have been too great. It would have crushed its lungs and killed it.

During the Age of Dinosaurs large reptiles could be found in the oceans as well as on the land. Plesiosaurs ('near lizard') were big sea creatures with short tails which were not much use for swimming. Instead they rowed using their broad, flat flippers. Some had long necks, others had short necks.

The long-necked type swam on the surface with its small head held above the water. It could flex its neck like the body of a snake. **Elasmosaurus** (1) was the largest known plesiosaur. About half of its 14 m (47 ft) length was its head and neck. The strange thing about this long-necked creature was

that it was unable to dive down. This was because it could not lift its four flippers higher than the shoulders and hips. When it saw a fish, it would stab down on its prey with its head.

The short-necked type had a large head with powerful jaws. In its huge mouth were dagger-like teeth. It could swim faster and farther than the long-necked creatures. To hunt for food it dived down to the deep. **Kronosaurus** (2) was 12 m (39 ft) long. Its head alone was longer than two men lying end to end.

Monsters in the air

By the Cretaceous Period there were not only monster dinosaurs roaming the land and fierce reptiles in the seas, there were also creatures in the air. They were not true birds. In fact, they evolved from the same group of reptiles that led to dinosaurs. They may have come from a small, tree-dwelling animal known as **podopteryx**. A web of skin linked the fore and hind limbs and the hind limbs with the base of the tail. Podopteryx used this skin to glide like present-day flying lizards and flying squirrels.

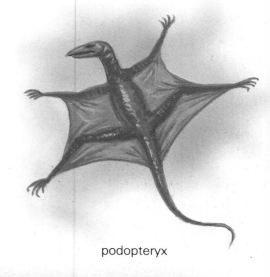

podopteryx

rhamphorhynchus in the air

The (pterosaurs) 'winged lizards' that evolved had a skeleton of thin, hollow bones. Each skin wing was fixed to the long bones of the arm and curved back to the hind legs. The muscles of many pterosaurs were too weak to flap their wings. They simply glided on currents of warm air. They swooped low to seize fish and small lizards. The long beak-like jaw was full of teeth.

Pterosaurs were clumsy on land because their legs were very short. They could only shuffle along. They probably hung upside down on cliffs or treetops to sleep – like bats. Here they were safe from enemies.

There were two main groups of pterosaurs. One group, the 'prow-beaks', used their long tail like a rudder. **Rhamphorhynchus** had a body only 45 cm (1½ ft) long. That is about the size of an eagle.

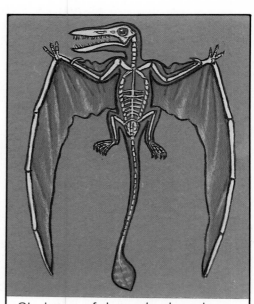

Skeleton of rhamphorhynchus – with wings attached to the extra long fourth finger of each hand.

The second group of pterosaurs were the pterodactyls. This name means 'winged fingers'. These creatures had long wings, little or no tail and a toothless beak. Some were as small as a sparrow, some were many times larger than an eagle.

Pteranodon was a pterodactyl with a wingspan of 7.6 m (25 ft). A fully-grown adult weighed 18 kg (40 lb). The skull of this flying reptile extended back into a long bony crest. This may have been used as a rudder to help it steer (instead of a tail) or to counterbalance the weight of the beak. From fossilised remains that have been found, scientists believe that the pteranodon flew as far as 100 km (62 miles) out over the sea. It scooped up fish in its long beak. Here is an adult pteranodon dropping fish from its mouth pouch to its young.

Quetzalcoatlus had a wingspan of over 12 m (39 ft), from tip to tip. This makes it the largest creature ever to have flown on Earth. No one knows how such a huge beast got up into the air. In 1975 fossil bones of this reptile were found in Texas, USA. As they were found inland it is possible that quetzalcoatlus was a kind of reptilian vulture that fed on dead animals.

How intelligent were the dinosaurs?

Most people think of dinosaurs as large, stupid animals and it is probably true that the larger ones were not very intelligent. They had tiny brains in comparison to their size.

The giant dinosaurs like brachiosaurus and diplodocus were over 23 m (75 ft) long but they had very small heads by comparison and their brains were no bigger than a kitten's. Some dinosaurs were thought to have had a second brain above the back legs but this was not really a brain, only a nerve centre to control the rear part of the animal.

Even dinosaurs with larger heads were no more intelligent. The pachycephalosaurus had a skull 60 cm (2 ft) long and 22 cm (8½ ins) thick but the brain inside did not even fill the space for it. Many of the carnivorous dinosaurs (e.g. allosaurus) had huge heads but these housed a large jaw system which enabled the dinosaurs to swallow whole pieces of flesh. Their heads were full of teeth not brains!

The most intelligent dinosaurs were probably the fast-moving 'ostrich' dinosaurs and the flying pterosaurs. They had the largest brains in comparison to their body size. Their agility and strong eyesight, needed for hunting and flying, also indicate their intelligence.

Intelligent or not, the dinosaurs did 'rule' the world for 160 million years.

Brachiosaurus – head the size of a horse's but a brain no bigger than a kitten's.

Pachycephalosaurus – 'head bangers' had thick skulls but not much inside.

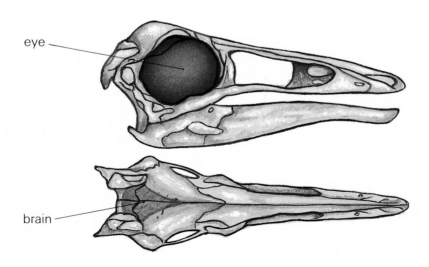

eye

brain

Dromiceiomimus – an 'ostrich' dinosaur with large eyes and a big brain.

Allosaurus – skull with rows of big, sharp teeth but not a very big brain.

Were they warm-blooded?

It is not known for certain whether dinosaurs were cold-blooded or warm-blooded. The reptiles of today are cold-blooded. This does not mean they have cold blood but that their body temperature varies with the air temperature. They rely on heat from the sun to warm their blood sufficiently to allow them to move freely. They shelter from the sun to cool down.

Birds and mammals, however, are warm-blooded. This means they maintain a constant body temperature. To achieve this, they eat more food when the weather is cold and when the weather is hot they lose heat by sweating or panting. Most warm-blooded animals have a covering of fur or feathers to help maintain their temperature.

There is a good case for thinking that the massive dinosaurs like brachiosaurus and diplodocus were cold-blooded. If they had been warm-blooded they would have had to spend all their time eating to maintain body temperature in such large bodies. It seems more likely that these slow movers were cold-blooded and gained heat by basking in the sun.

Another group of dinosaurs which probably used the sun to warm their blood were the spinosaurs. The **spinosaurus** had spines along its back that held a kind of sail of skin through which blood flowed. If it stood sideways to the sun at dawn (a) it could use its 'sail' as a 'solar panel' quickly warming its blood and making it active. When the sun became too hot at midday, the spinosaurus could lose heat by standing with its back to the sun (b).

On the other hand, many of the smaller dinosaurs like compsognathus, deinonychus and the 'ostrich' dinosaurs (e.g. **saurornithoides**) had erect postures, long limbs and were fast movers. As only warm-blooded creatures tend to move quickly, this suggests these animals were warm-blooded. Evidence also suggests that certain of these dinosaurs hunted at night, a time when cold-blooded creatures would be inactive.

a

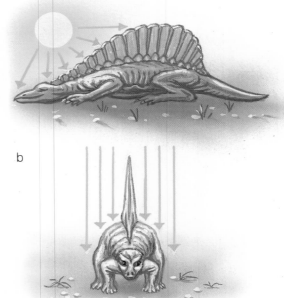

b

saurornithoides

Why did dinosaurs die out?

About 65 million years ago dinosaurs vanished from the face of the Earth. This may have taken anything from a few years to five million years. Experts cannot agree on this. Why did this happen to a group of animals that had ruled so successfully for so long? It was not only the land-living dinosaurs that died out but also the monsters in the air and the monsters of the deep. Many other land and sea creatures also died out. However, snakes, lizards, crocodiles, frogs, toads, salamanders, birds and some mammals survived.

Many theories have been suggested. Here are some of them. None of these theories has been proved correct.

Was it a natural disaster such as a flood, earthquake or volcano eruption? This is unlikely because all forms of life would have been affected.

Egg thieves may have stolen all the eggs so that no young were born.

Perhaps carnivores ate all the plant-eaters and then ate each other.

Did the dinosaurs grow so large that they could not breed or move?

Did new flowering plants poison them?

Did a plague of caterpillars strip the leaves from trees?

Did their diet make the dinosaurs lay soft-shelled eggs that did not hatch?

A rock — 10 km (6 miles) across — may have streaked from space and hit the Earth. The impact could have hurled dust and moisture up into the atmosphere, darkening the sky for months and killing all the vegetation.

The theory that makes the most sense is the one that suggests there was a sudden and dramatic change of climate. The theory is that winters became very much colder. If dinosaurs were warm-blooded, they lacked fur or feathers to trap their body heat. If they were cold-blooded, many dinosaurs were too big to hibernate in frost-free holes. The cold would have killed many plants leaving less food for plant-eating dinosaurs. If these died from starvation, there would have been fewer dinosaurs for the flesh-eaters to prey on and they too would starve to death. A similar fate would have been in store for the monsters in the seas. Flying monsters would have suffered too. A drop in temperature at the poles would have led to an increase in wind strengths and speeds. These creatures were gliders, not flappers. They would have lost control in stronger winds and crashed to the ground.

The vanishing dinosaurs remains one of the great mysteries. Whatever the reason, it is sad that these exciting and fascinating creatures who ruled for 160 million years had to die out. When the Age of Dinosaurs ended, the Age of Mammals began.

Finding out about fossils

When creatures die their bodies usually rot. No trace is left. Sometimes, however, the hard parts are preserved in rock as fossils. These are formed in several ways. When a dinosaur drowned, it floated down river and lodged on a sandbank in the shallows of the river (1). Its flesh and skin soon rotted, exposing the bones (2). Before its bones decayed, mud or sand covered them (3). This shut out the oxygen needed by the bacteria that cause decay. Minerals from the water seeped into the bones and hardened them.

Not all fossils formed under water. Some were buried under sand in the deserts. Sometimes bones dissolved, leaving hollows that showed their shape. These fossils are known as moulds. If minerals fill a mould they form a cast (see below).

The crushing weight of many layers above the bones changed the mud or sand layers into beds of rock (4). Millions of years later, great movements of the Earth's crust may have thrust up these layers to build high mountains. Rain and frost began to wear down the mountains. Slowly, over thousands of years, the weather bares the fossil bones (5).

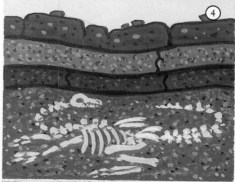

Often only scattered fossil bones survive. This is probably because they are the remains of corpses torn apart by scavengers or by floods. Even a single fossilised bone can provide useful clues to the size, shape and movement of a dinosaur.

A fossil **mould** is produced when dinosaur bones dissolve to leave hollows in the rock that formed around them. The hollows are in the shape of the bones.

A **cast** is produced when the hollow in the mould is filled by minerals. This is similar to making a plaster cast – only it takes a great deal longer!

Apart from bones, other fossilised remains help us to understand more about the lives of creatures living in the Age of Dinosaurs. Footprints made in soft mud are preserved as fossils if the mud hardened into rock before rain or running water washed away the prints. Teeth are important because they provide information about how the dinosaur ate – whether it chewed, sawed or ripped its food. Fossilised dinosaur droppings tell us what the creature ate. Skin or the marks left by skin survive from some dinosaurs, usually those that died in dry conditions. The fossilised eggs of some dinosaurs have also survived.

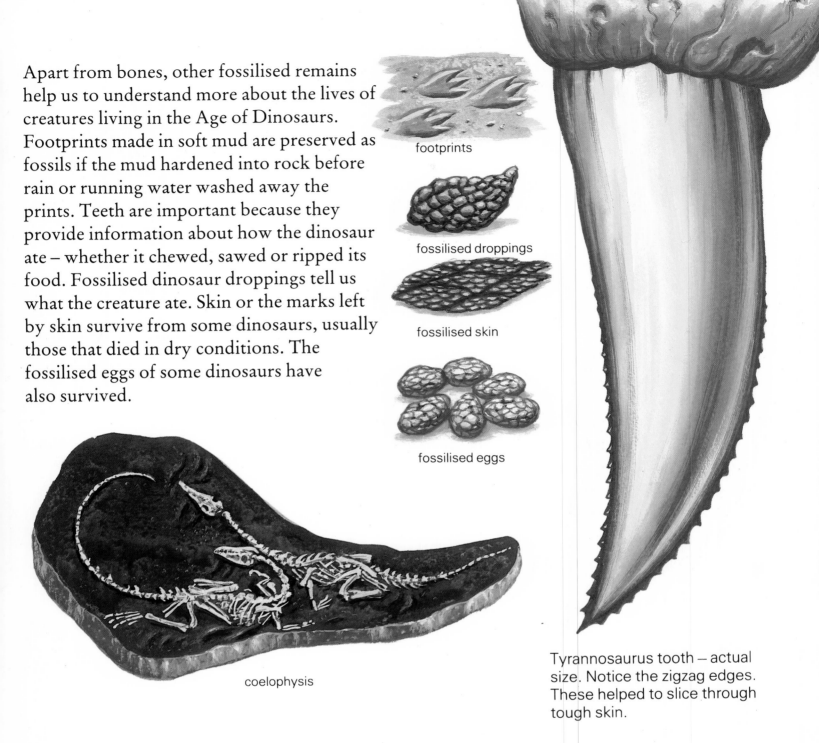

footprints

fossilised droppings

fossilised skin

fossilised eggs

coelophysis

Tyrannosaurus tooth — actual size. Notice the zigzag edges. These helped to slice through tough skin.

Cannibal dinosaur

In 1947 fossil hunters uncovered an amazing collection of fossil bones in New Mexico, USA. Dozens of skeletons of a dinosaur known as **coelophysis** were buried in a cliff. The bones were packed on top of each other. It looked as if these creatures lived and died together. Perhaps they were smothered by a landfall or sandstorm. Scientists were able to rebuild the dinosaurs. Two skeletons contained the tiny bones of young of the same type of dinosaur inside the rib cage. This may have meant that the coelophysis gave birth to live young but it is more likely that it was a cannibal dinosaur. When hungry, coelophysis would catch and cram into its jaws any prey that happened to be near. This included smaller members of its own kind.

Digging up a dinosaur

How do fossil hunters find the remains of dinosaurs? In the early years of fossil hunting many finds were made by accident. Now the experts know the most likely places. It is rare for bones to be lying around ready to be put straight into a bag or box. They are often found in cliffs and quarries. New dinosaurs are still being found and a recent find in a Surrey clay pit in 1983 has been named baryonyx walkeri ('heavy clawed creature found by Mr Walker'). This unique carnivorous dinosaur species had 128 teeth instead of the usual 64, and is believed to have preyed on fish.

When fossil remains are found, notes are made of where they were found. Then begins the task of removing the fossils. The soil and rock are removed until half the bone is exposed (1). Foil or wet tissue paper is wrapped round the bone (2). Then foam or plaster of Paris is added. This hardens to form a protective casing (3). Next they dig away the surrounding soil, turn the bone over and wrap the other half. Small fossils are placed in bags and large ones in crates (4).

The fossils are then cleaned. This may take years. First scientists soak, saw or slice away the foam or plaster bandages. Weak areas of exposed bone are hardened with special chemicals. Hard rock is chipped away with hammer and chisel. A dentist's drill is often used to speed up the work.

Scientists then rebuild the skeleton of the dinosaur, with missing pieces rebuilt in glass fibre.

stegosaurus skeleton

apatosaurus skeleton

In the museum

Natural history museums often produce life-size copies of dinosaur skeletons. They make plaster moulds of the bones and fill these with glass fibre to form casts. The skeleton of one of the giant dinosaurs often fills an entire hall in a museum. Whole scenes showing dinosaurs and landscapes are recreated as realistically as possible to help you understand more about the exciting creatures that lived on the Earth so many millions of years ago.

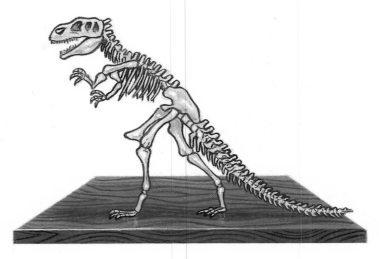

allosaurus skeleton

TRICERATOPS

Index

The numbers in circles refer to the map of the world as it is today – on the next page. The numbers that follow are page references.
In the case of the dinosaurs, a translation of the name is given in *italic* followed by a short description of the animal.

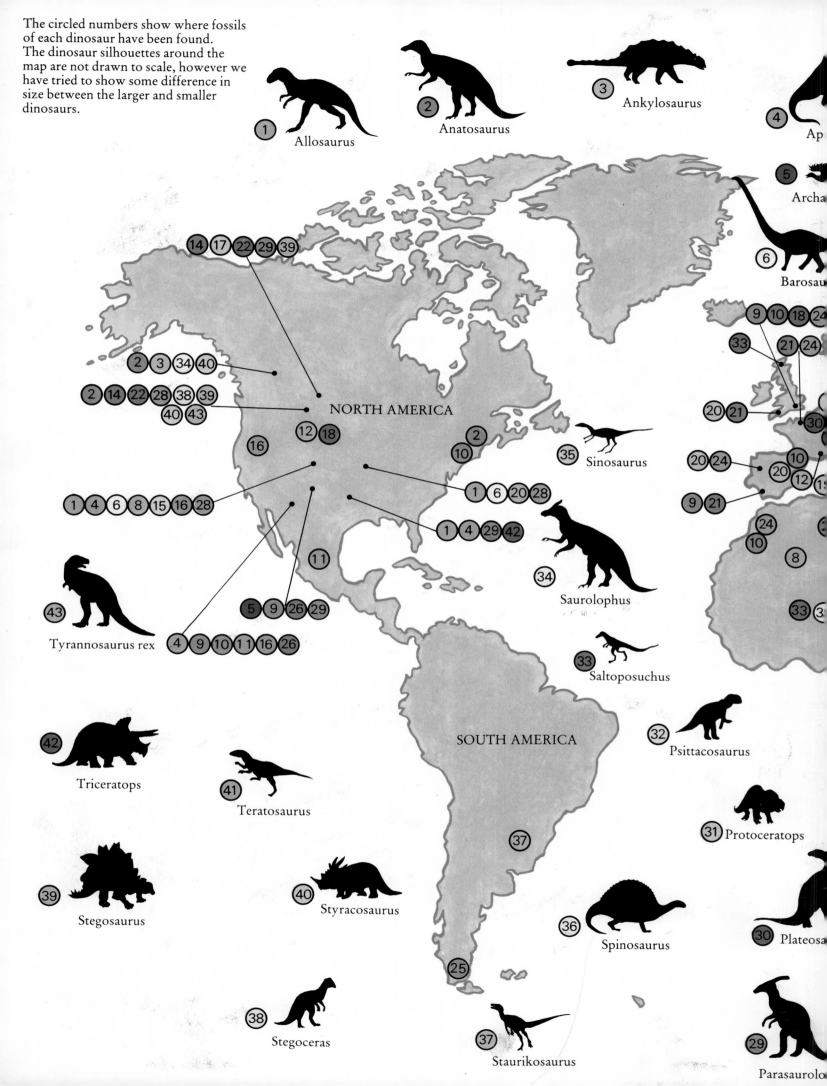

The circled numbers show where fossils of each dinosaur have been found. The dinosaur silhouettes around the map are not drawn to scale, however we have tried to show some difference in size between the larger and smaller dinosaurs.

① Allosaurus

② Anatosaurus

③ Ankylosaurus

④ Ap

⑤ Archa

⑥ Barosau

NORTH AMERICA

⑭ ⑰ ㉒ ㉙ ㊴

② ③ ㉞ ㊵

② ⑭ ㉒ ㉘ ㊳ ㊴ ㊵ ㊸

⑫ ⑱

⑯

② ⑩

⑨ ⑩ ⑱ ㉔

㉝ ㉑ ㉔

⑳ ㉑

⑳ ㉔ ⑩ ⑳ ⑫

⑨ ㉑ ㉚

① ④ ⑥ ⑧ ⑮ ⑯ ㉘

① ⑥ ⑳ ㉘

① ④ ㉙ ㊷

⑪

⑤ ⑨ ㉖ ㉙

④ ⑨ ⑩ ⑪ ⑯ ㉖

㊸ Tyrannosaurus rex

㉟ Sinosaurus

㉔ ⑩ ⑧

㉝

㉞ Saurolophus

㉝ Saltoposuchus

㉝ Psittacosaurus

㉜ Psittacosaurus

SOUTH AMERICA

㊷

㉛ Protoceratops

㊷

㊵ Styracosaurus

㊱ Spinosaurus

㉚ Plateosa

㉕

㊳ Stegoceras

㊲ Staurikosaurus

㊴ Stegosaurus

㊴ Styracosaurus

㊷ Protoceratops

㊷ Staurikosaurus

㉙ Parasaurolo

㊷ Teratosaurus

㊷ Triceratops

㊷ Stegoceras